# I want to be a Firefighter

# I WANT TO BE A
# Firefighter

FIREFLY BOOKS

# A Firefly Book

Published by Firefly Books Ltd. 1999

Third Printing, 2002

**National Library of Canada Cataloguing in Publication Data**

Main entry under title:

I want to be a firefighter

ISBN 1-55209-448-0 (bound)
ISBN 1-55209-433-2 (pbk.)

1. Fire extinction – Juvenile literature.
2. Fire fighters – Juvenile literature.

TH9148/I25 1999   j363.37   C99-930932-3

Published in Canada in 1999 by
Firefly Books Ltd.
3680 Victoria Park Avenue
Toronto, Ontario, Canada  M2H 3K1

**Library of Congress Cataloguing-in-Publication Data**

I want to be a firefighter / Firefly Books Ltd.].–1st ed.
[24] p. : col. Ill. ; cm. –I want to be.
Summary : Photos and easy-to-read text about the job of a firefighter.

ISBN 1-55209-448-0 (bound)
ISBN 1-55209-433-2 (pbk.)

1. Fire fighters– Vocational guidance – Juvenile literature. [1. Fire fighters – Vocational guidance. 2. Occupations.] I. Title. II. Series.
331.761/3633–dc21    1999    AC   CIP

Published in the United States in 1999 by
Firefly Books (U.S.) Inc.
P.O. Box 1338, Ellicott Station
Buffalo, New York, USA  14205

**Photo Credits**
© Al Harvey, pages 5, 6, 16-17, 18, 20
© Michael Salas/The Image Bank, front cover
© Patti McConville/The Image Bank, page 7
© Jay Silverman/The Image Bank, page 24
© William Edwards/The Image Bank, back cover
© COMSTOCK/Bill Wittman, page 11
© COMSTOCK, pages 8-9

© Masterfile/Bob Anderson, page 10
© Masterfile/Douglas Walker, pages 12-13
© Masterfile/Mike Dobel, page 14
© Masterfile/Edward Gifford, page 15
© Masterfile/Mark Tomalty, page 19
© Masterfile/Sherman Hines, page 21
© Masterfile/Elmar Krenkel, pages 22-23

Design by Interrobang Graphic Design Inc.
Printed and bound in Canada

*The Publisher acknowledges the financial support of the Government of Canada through the Book Publishing Industry Development Program for its publishing activities.*

Firefighters must come to the rescue quickly when there is a fire. They drive trucks called fire engines.

The fire engine carries a powerful hose and a long ladder. It has a siren to use when there is a fire. Have you heard the noise fire engines make?

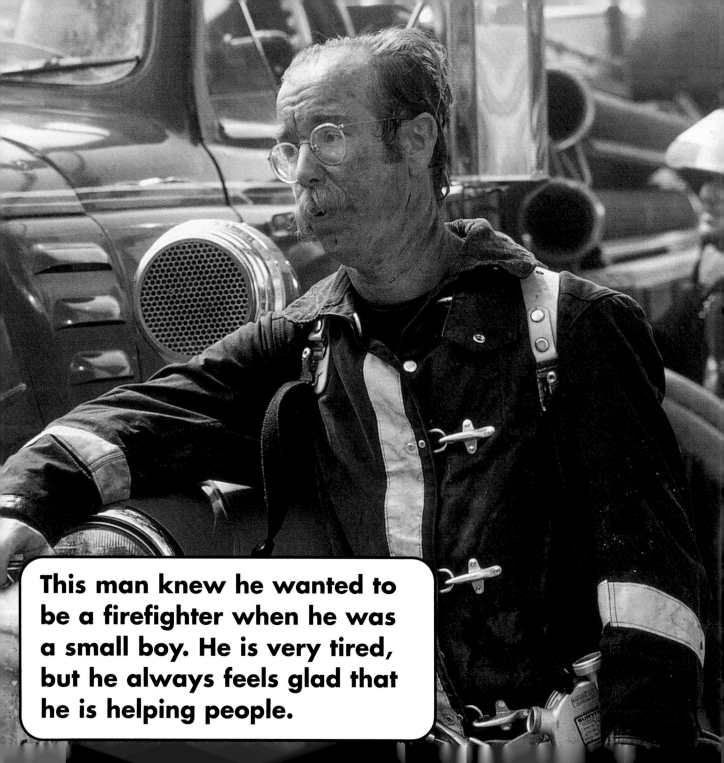

This man knew he wanted to be a firefighter when he was a small boy. He is very tired, but he always feels glad that he is helping people.

Firefighters must be strong to carry the heavy equipment and control the powerful fire hoses.

The hose sprays water into the middle of the flames. The firefighters must hold on tightly!

Fires can happen at any time. Sometimes firefighters must work all night.

The smoke from a fire can make people sick, so firefighters carry tanks of fresh air to breathe.

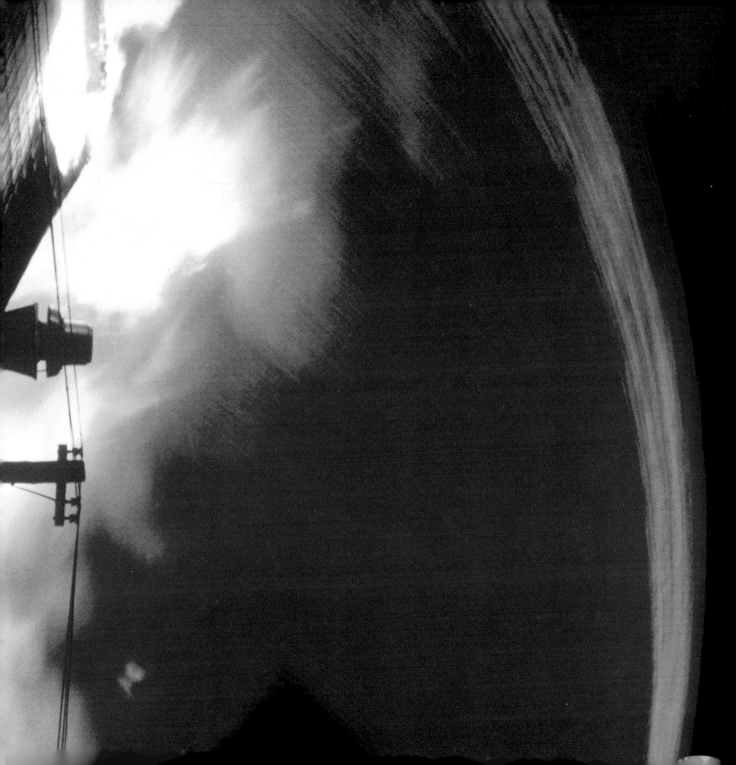

Firefighters make sure everyone is safe. Sometimes firefighters are hurt while helping other people.

Sometimes cars catch fire. Although the fire is small, these firefighters are careful to protect their bodies with thick coats.

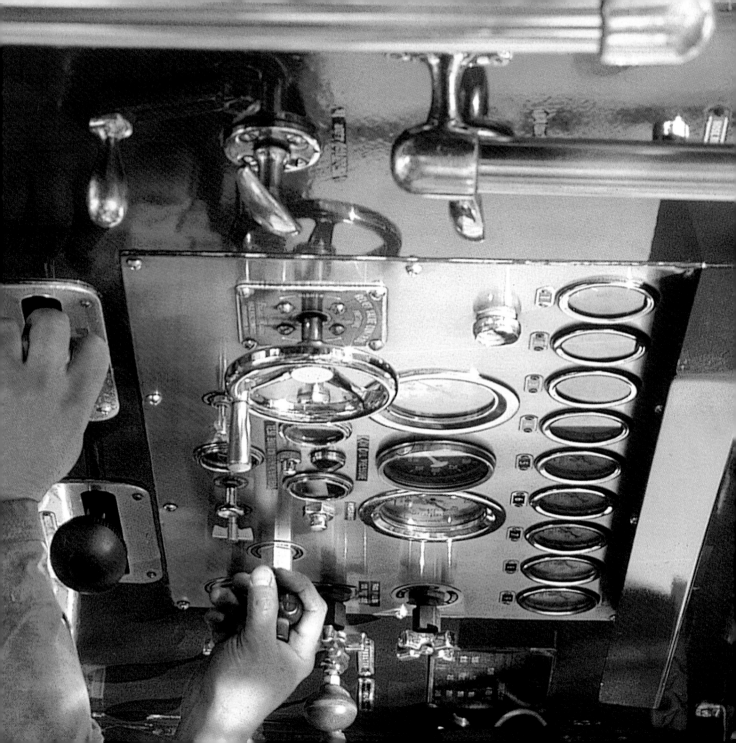

When there are no fires, firefighters wait at the firehouse. They make sure their equipment is clean and works properly.

This fire was hard to reach from the ground, so the firefighter sprays water down on it from high above.

Sometimes fires start on boats or ships, or on buildings near the water. Fireboat to the rescue!

Helicopters can dump water over large areas. That's important because forest fires spread quickly.